AGUSTINIA

and Other Dinosaurs of
Central and South America

by Dougal Dixon

illustrated by
Steve Weston and James Field

PICTURE WINDOW BOOKS
Minneapolis, Minnesota

Types of dinosaurs

In this book, a red shape at the top of a left-hand page shows the animal was a meat-eater. A green shape shows it was a plant-eater.

Just how big—or small— were they?

Dinosaurs were many different sizes. We have compared their size to one of the following:

Chicken
2 feet (60 centimeters) tall
Weight 6 pounds (2.7 kilograms)

Adult person
6 feet (1.8 meters) tall
Weight 170 pounds (76.5 kg)

Elephant
10 feet (3 m) tall
Weight 12,000 pounds
(5,400 kg)

Picture Window Books
5115 Excelsior Boulevard
Suite 232
Minneapolis, MN 55416
877-845-8392
www.picturewindowbooks.com

Printed in the United States of America.

Library of Congress Cataloging-in-Publication Data
Dixon, Dougal.
Agustinia and other dinosaurs of Central and South America / by Dougal Dixon ; illustrated by Steve Weston & James Field.
p. cm. — (Dinosaur find)
Includes bibliographical references and index.
ISBN-13: 978-1-4048-2263-4 (library binding)
ISBN-10: 1-4048-2263-1 (library binding)
ISBN-13: 978-1-4048-2269-6 (paperback)
ISBN-10: 1-4048-2269-0 (paperback)
1. Dinosaurs—Central America—Juvenile literature.
2. Dinosaurs—South America—Juvenile literature.
I. Weston, Steve, ill. II. Field, James, 1959- ill.
III. Title.
QE861.5.D58 2007
567.9098—dc22   2006027942

Acknowledgments
This book was produced for Picture Window Books by Bender Richardson White, U.K.

Illustrations by James Field (pages 4-5, 11, 13, 15) and Steve Weston (cover pages 1, 7, 9, 17, 21). Diagrams by Stefan Chabluk.

Photographs: Digital Vision pages 8, 10. Getty Images page 16. istockphotos pages 6 (Steffen Foerster), 12 (Jurie Maree), 14 (Mike Bentley), 18 (Andrew Howe), 20 (Cay-Uwe Kulzer).

Consultant: John Stidworthy, Scientific Fellow of the Zoological Society, London, and former Lecturer in the Education Department, Natural History Museum, London.

Reading Adviser: Susan Kesselring, M.A., Literacy Educator, Rosemount-Apple Valley-Eagan (Minnesota) School District

TABLE OF CONTENTS

WHAT'S INSIDE?

Dinosaurs! These dinosaurs lived in places that now form Central America and South America. Find out how they survived millions of years ago and what they have in common with today's animals.

LIFE IN CENTRAL AND SOUTH AMERICA

Dinosaurs lived between 230 million and 65 million years ago. The world did not look the same then. Much of the land and many of the seas were not in the same places as today. For much of the time, South America was not joined to Central and North America. Different types of dinosaurs lived in each area.

A herd of *Bonitasaura* walked across the plains. At their feet ran small *Alvarezsaurus*. In the distance, two *Aucasaurus* got ready to charge, looking for any easy kill.

BUITRERAPTOR

Pronunciation:
BEW-tier-RAP-tur

With feathered arms and tail, the little, bird-like *Buitreraptor* pecked around in the undergrowth for small animals to eat. It hunted for snakes, lizards, and insects. Using long jaws full of sharp little teeth, it would grab and hold prey.

Feathered hunter today

The modern secretary bird is about the size of *Buitreraptor*. It hunts for the same kind of prey, including snakes.

Size Comparison

With sharp eyesight and long jaws, *Buitreraptor* could easily catch and eat small but dangerous animals such as snakes.

AGUSTINIA

Pronunciation:
AG-us-TIN-ee-uh

The strange thing about *Agustinia* were the plates along its back. Some of the plates were leaf-shaped. Others were like spikes. They made *Agustinia* look larger than it was. Most other long-necked, plant-eating dinosaurs did not have any structures like these.

Size and signals today

To look bigger, modern bears stand on their hind legs when they must defend themselves. *Agustinia* may have used its plates in a similar way, hoping to scare off attackers.

Size Comparison

The plates along the neck, back, and tail of Agustinia were used for protection and to signal to the other members of the herd.

AUCASAURUS

Pronunciation:
AW-ka-SAW-rus

Aucasaurus hunted herds of big plant-eating dinosaurs that roamed the plains. Using strong back legs, it charged at prey. After separating an animal from the herd, Aucasaurus went in for the kill. It used strong jaws and sawlike teeth to cut open the prey's neck.

Killing jaws today

The modern leopard charges at prey and kills with powerful jaws, like Aucasaurus once did.

Size Comparison

Aucasaurus stood on high ground to watch the passing herds of plant-eaters. When it saw a slow-moving animal, Aucasaurus moved onto the plains to chase the prey.

ALVAREZSAURUS

Pronunciation:
AL-vuh-rez-SAW-rus

Long-legged and long-tailed
Alvarezsaurus ran across the plains.
It may have been an anteater,
digging into ant nests with the
strong, single claws on its hands.
After pulling the ants from a nest,
Alvarezsaurus would have popped
them into its little jaws.

Long legs today

The modern ostrich uses
long legs to run away
from trouble, much like
Alvarezsaurus did.

Size Comparison

Turkey-sized Alvarezsaurus moved around quickly, keeping their eyes open for meat-eaters that wanted to catch and eat them.

BONITASAURA

Pronunciation:
BON-ee-tuh-SAW-ruh

Bonitasaura had jaws that were broad and straight at the front and armed with teeth for grabbing plants. This big dinosaur must have been able to pull up huge mouthfuls of low-growing plants to eat.

Flat-fronted jaws today

The modern cow pulls up grass and eats it like *Bonitasaura* did. This is because the cow has jaws like those of *Bonitasaura*.

Size Comparison

Bonitasaura was a long-necked plant-eater. It pulled plants from the ground with its front teeth and chopped the food with its side teeth.

EORAPTOR

Pronunciation:
EE-o-RAP-tur

Eoraptor was one of the first dinosaurs. It was a duck-sized meat-eater that ran on its hind legs and ate insects, lizards, and small mammals. Over millions of years, little dinosaurs such as *Eoraptor* evolved into many different types of giant dinosaurs.

Dinosaur-like animals today

Modern birds came from the same animals that dinosaurs did. Birds look more like the tiny early dinosaurs than the big ones that came later.

Size Comparison

Using sure feet and sharp eyesight, *Eoraptor* hunted small lizards.

SALTASAURUS

Pronunciation:
SALT-a-SAW-rus

Saltasaurus was a long-necked plant-eater with armor on its back. These dinosaurs made nests and lived in herds. Predators attacked the nests to eat the eggs and young. The adult *Saltasaurus* were protected from predators by armor.

Nesting together today

Terns nest together on open ground, just as *Saltasaurus* did. This helps to keep them safe.

Size Comparison

Saltasaurus made a nest by scraping together sand and dirt. It laid eggs in a hollow space in the middle of the nest.

GASPARINASAURA

Pronunciation:
GAS-pih-RIN-uh-SAW-ruh

Among dinosaurs, not only the small meat-eaters were fast runners. *Gasparinasaura* was a speedy plant-eater. It fed on low-growing plants. When any of the larger meat-eaters came along, it dashed to safety on its long hind legs.

Low plant feeders today

The modern goose feeds on low-growing plants, just as *Gasparinasaura* did.

Size Comparison

Gasparinasaura fed mainly on ferns growing in the forests. These dinosaurs moved and rested in small groups.

Where Did They Go?

Dinosaurs are extinct, which means that none of them are alive today. Scientists study rocks and fossils to find clues about what happened to dinosaurs.

People have different explanations about what happened. Some people think a huge asteroid hit Earth and caused all sorts of climate changes, which caused the dinosaurs to die. Others think volcanic eruptions caused the climate to change and that killed the dinosaurs. No one knows for sure what happened to all of the dinosaurs.

GLOSSARY

armor—protective covering of plates, horns, spikes, or clubs used for fighting

evolve—to change gradually, especially concerning animals and plants

ferns—plants with finely divided leaves known as fronds; ferns are common in damp woods and along rivers

fossils—the remains of a plant or animal that lived between thousands and millions of years ago

herds—large groups of animals that move, feed, and sleep together

mammals—warm-blooded animals that have hair and drink mother's milk when they are young

plains—large areas of flat land with few large plants

plate—a large, flat, usually tough structure on the body

prey—animals that are hunted by other animals for food; the hunters are known as predators

signal—to make a sign, warning, or hint

To Learn More

At the Library

Clark, Neil, and William Lindsay. *1001 Facts About Dinosaurs.* New York: Backpack Books, Dorling Kindersley, 2002.

Dixon, Dougal. *Dougal Dixon's Amazing Dinosaurs.* Honesdale, Pa.: Boyds Mills Press, 2000.

Holtz, Thomas, and Michael Brett-Surman. *Dinosaur Field Guide.* New York: Random House, 2001.

On the Web

FactHound offers a safe, fun way to find Web sites related to this book. All of the sites on FactHound have been researched by our staff.

1. Visit *www.facthound.com*
2. Type in this special code: 1404822631
3. Click on the FETCH IT button.

Your trusty FactHound will fetch the best Web sites for you!

Index

Look for all of the books in the Dinosaur Find series:

Agustinia and Other Dinosaurs of Central and South America

Aletopelta and Other Dinosaurs of the West Coast

Allosaurus and Other Dinosaurs of the Rockies

Ankylosaurus and Other Mountain Dinosaurs

Centrosaurus and Other Dinosaurs of Cold Places

Ceratosaurus and Other Fierce Dinosaurs

Coelophysis and Other Dinosaurs of the South

Deltadromeus and Other Shoreline Dinosaurs

Dromaeosaurus and Other Dinosaurs of the North

Giganotosaurus and Other Big Dinosaurs

Maiasaura and Other Dinosaurs of the Midwest

Minmi and Other Dinosaurs of Australia

Neovenator and Other Dinosaurs of Europe

Nodosaurus and Other Dinosaurs of the East Coast

Ornithomimus and Other Fast Dinosaurs

Plateosaurus and Other Desert Dinosaurs

Saltopus and Other First Dinosaurs

Scutellosaurus and Other Small Dinosaurs

Spinosaurus and Other Dinosaurs of Africa

Stegosaurus and Other Plains Dinosaurs

Styracosaurus and Other Last Dinosaurs

Therizinosaurus and Other Dinosaurs of Asia

Triceratops and Other Forest Dinosaurs

Tyrannosaurus and Other Dinosaurs of North America